BOOK I

WOHLFAHRT

FOUNDATION STUDIES

FOR THE

VIOLIN

Selected, Edited, and Arranged
in Progressive Order by

K. H. AIQOUNI

Book I (O2465) - 60 First Position Studies (from Opus 45, 54, 74)

Book II (O2466) - 42 Studies - First, Second, and Third Positions
(from Opus 45 and 74)

CARL FISCHER®

65 Bleecker Street, New York, NY 10012

O2465

ISBN 0-8258-0144-3

Preface

The present edition has been prepared with a definite, threefold object.

First, to select the most serviceable first position studies from each of F. Wohlfahrt's five books (Op. 45 Nos. I and II, 54, 74 Nos. I and II), to re-arrange their order as to grade of difficulty, style, etc., and in addition to maintain a better and more logical relationship as regards tonality than exists in previous original editions.

Second, to include only such of the studies as will prove of greatest importance for the student *at this particular stage* of his technical development.

Third, to provide a more thorough and consistent system of fingering and bowing marks for the studies, and to call attention to certain points, which the editor, in the course of his long teaching experience, has found troublesome and difficult for young students.

Small dashes over two notes indicate the change of strings at that point. The finger taking the first note should be kept down while the right hand effects the transition of the bow from one string to the other. A long dash indicates that the finger taking that note, is to be kept down throughout. Small dashes are only used ɲ the first twenty studies. Some of the studies have been provided with several varieties of bowing and the teacher should insist that the student work out each one of them thoroughly, before passing on to the next study.

All the studies should be practiced slowly at the beginning, regardless of the prescribed tempo indications; those with complicated bowing are preceded by preparatory exercises on the open A string. They are to be practiced on all strings until the bow arm has become used to the necessary movements. This plan, faithfully followed, will save the student much valuable time and a great deal of wasted effort.

In conclusion it may be mentioned that this new compilation of Franz Wohlfahrt's excellent study material, edited as above described and available in two books, should prove both welcome and serviceable for all foundation work.

THE EDITOR

Thematic List of the Studies

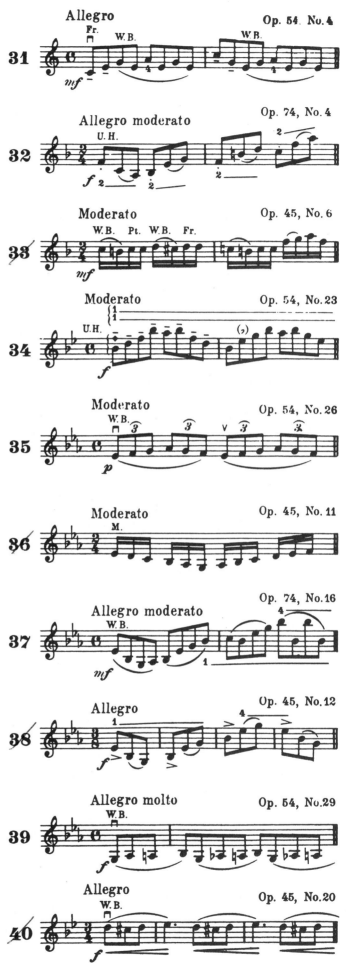

Sixty First Position Studies
for Violin

by FRANZ WOHLFAHRT
(Foundation Studies)

Selected, Edited and
Arranged in Progressive Order
by K. H. AIQOUNI

Book I

W. B. = Whole Bow
M. = Middle Bow
Pt. = At the point
Fr. = At the heel (frog)

U. H. = Upper Half
L. H. = Lower Half
⊓ = Down Bow
V = Up Bow

All strings to be played open unless marked (4)

Variants

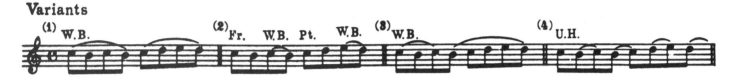

(1) W.B.   (2) Fr. W.B. Pt. W.B.   (3) W.B.   (4) U.H.

IMPORTANT REMARK: The student should bear in mind that, when playing the notes located on the same string the finger or fingers taking these notes should be kept down *as long as possible.*

Op. 45, No. 1

Allegro moderato

Largo
W.B.
Op. 45, No.8

Slower and W.B. for each note

Moderato
U.H.
Op. 45, No.3

4

Allegretto

Op. 45, No. 4

At N.B. The quarter note gets two full beats.

★) This A is located a half tone lower on the E string than the D♯ in the preceding measure on the A string.

During this study the fingers should be kept down as long as possible.

At all the skips, the fingers between the finger taking the lower, and the one taking the higher note, should be brought down on the string with the latter.

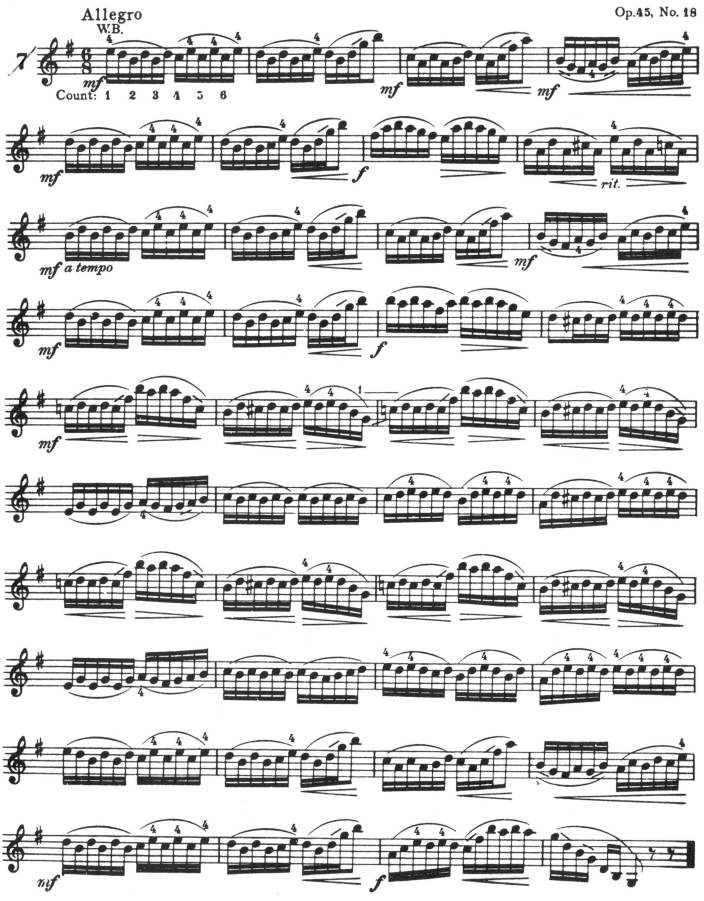

Allegro

Op.45, No. 18

Count: 1 2 3 4 5 6

Allegro moderato

8

This study should be played with four beats to a measure. The eighth notes in the second measure get one beat each played with full, sweeping strokes.

Variants

Op.54, No.1

Allegro moderato

12

Op 45, No. 16

Moderato
W. B.

13

mf

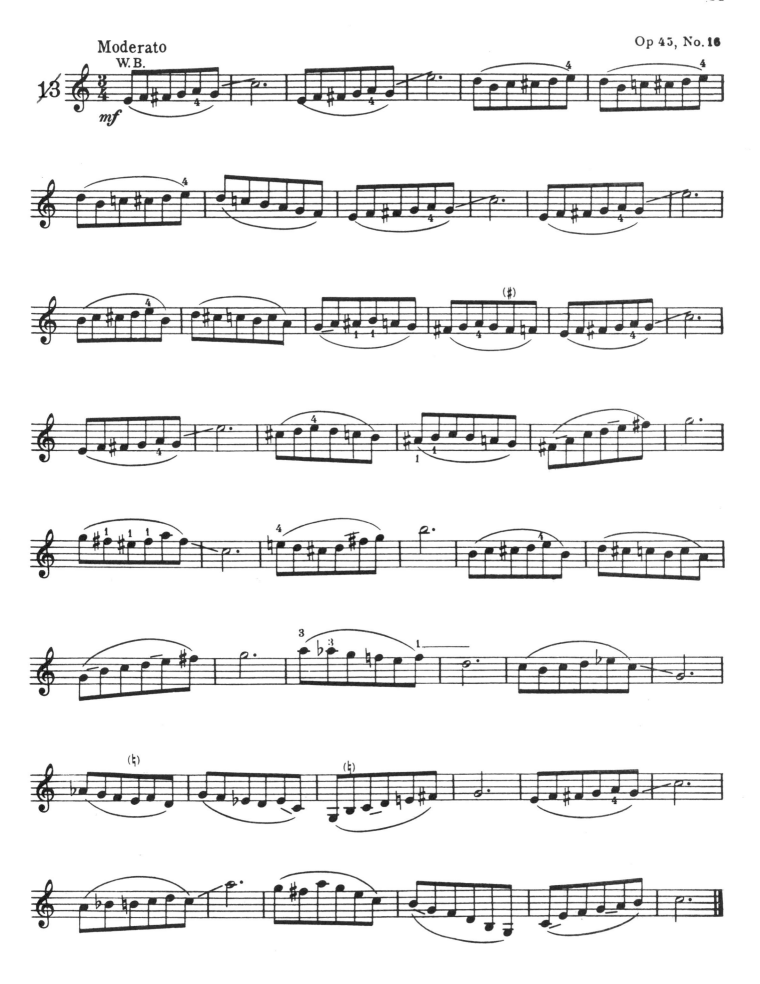

Variants

Op. 74 No. 2

Allegro moderato

14

Allegro non tanto

Op. 43, No. 14

15

*) This "C♯" is located a half tone higher on the A string, than the preceding "G" on the E string. This fact should be born in mind throughout this study.

**) The notes under the brackets (⌐) should be covered at once with the same finger.

Op. 43, No. 9

Allegretto

16

Preparatory Exercise for No.17

Count slowly: 1 2 3 1 2 3

Raise the bow off the string
during the rests.

Allegro moderato

Op. 54, No. 9

17

Allegro

Op. 54, No. 14

18

Count: 1 2 3 4 1 2 3 4

Variants
(1) L.H.   (2) W.B.

Op. 74, No. 6

Allegro moderato

19

At N.B. Cover F# and B with the first finger throughout as indicated.

24744-56

This study if **found too** difficult at first should be practiced with notes ~~separated~~ (at the M.) beginning the first note with the up bow.

Allegro

Op. 45, No. **22**

20

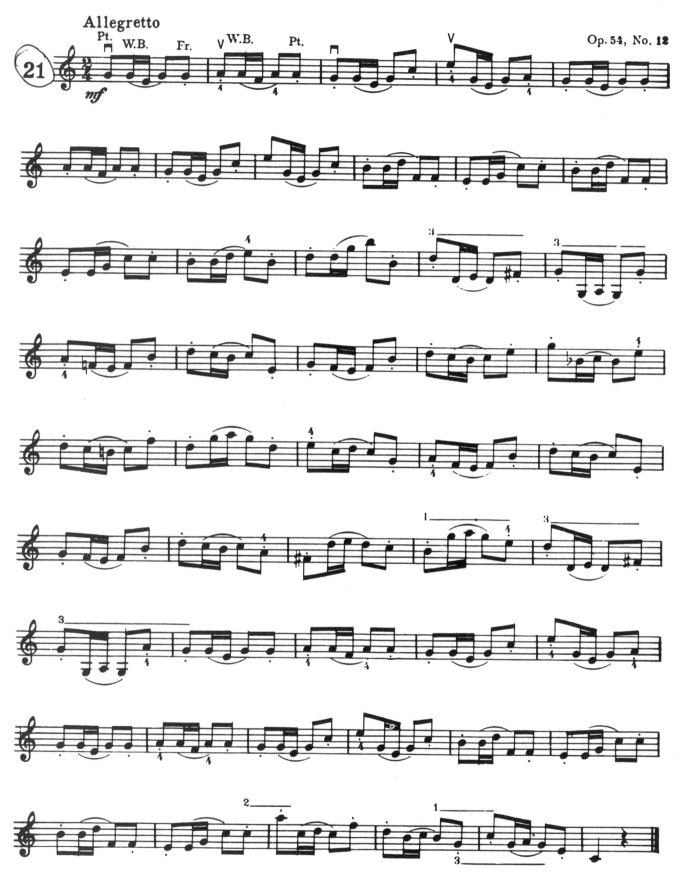

18

Practice slowly at first using the W. B. for the slurred notes, and taking the separate ones at the Pt. and at the Fr.

Op. 74, No. 8

At N.B: This quarter note gets the time of *four sixteenth notes.*

24744-56

NOTE: From this number on, the passages that are repeated are marked only once. The student should remember and use the same fingering at each recurrence.

Allegro
W.B.

Op. 74, No. 10

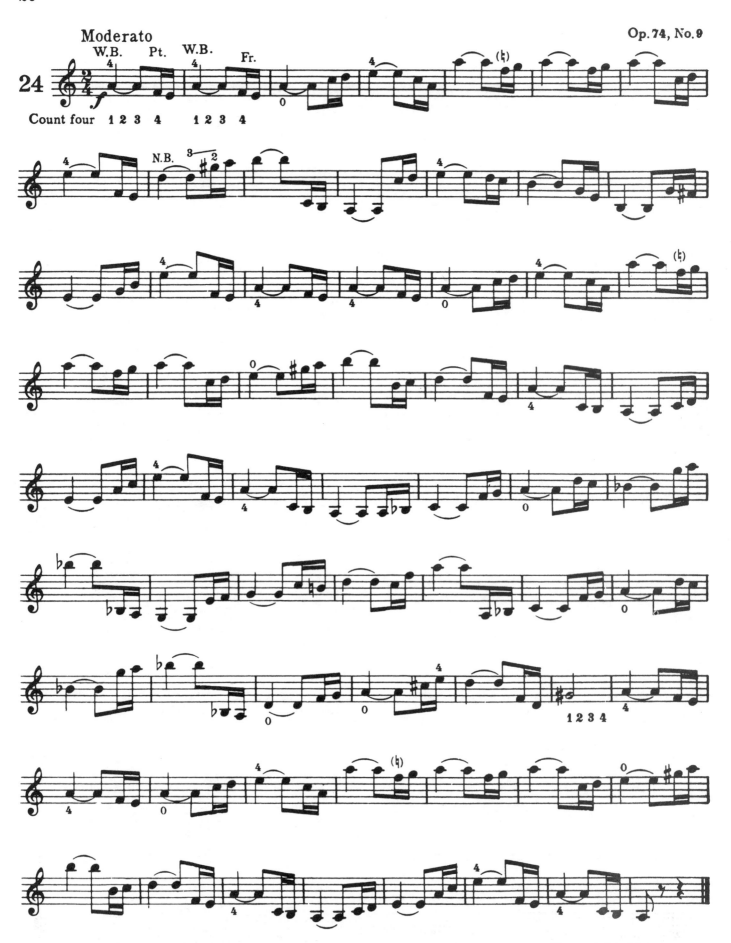

The "G♯" in the measure marked N.B. is located one half tone away from "D".

This is an excellent study for the fourth finger: All "A"s and "E"s, unless marked otherwise are to be played with the fourth finger.

3/27

Moderato
W. B.

Op. 54, No. 10

25

p

22

Preparatory Exercise for No. 26

W.B. W.B. Fr.   W.B. W.B. Fr.

1   2 3 4   1   2 3 4

Lift the bow off the string during the eighth rests where ever they occur.

Allegro

Op. 54, No. 8

26

Op. 54, No. 11

27

Allegro
W.B.*(a)*

Op. 54, No. 22

(a) Also put down the second finger on the string every time G is played with the third.
(b) Put the third finger down with the fourth. *(c)* All the three fingers to be raised and put down together.
(d) All the four fingers to be put down and raised together.

24744-56

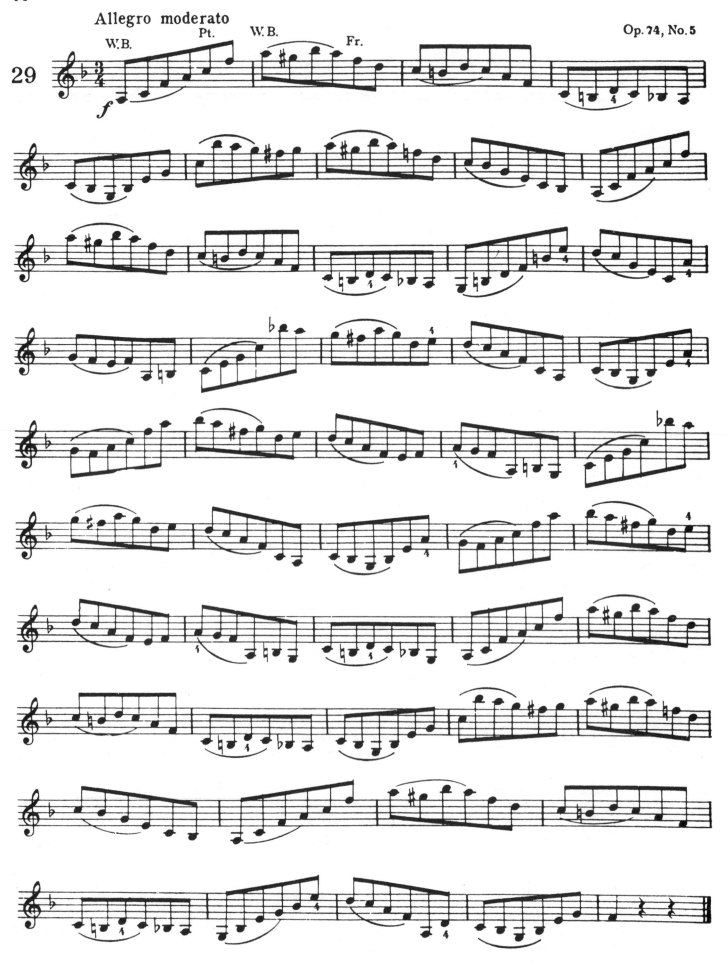

24

Allegro moderato

Op. 74, No. 5

29

To be practiced both with the L. H. and the U. H. for each stroke.   Count four in a measure.

Op. 74, No. 14

Allegretto

30

mf

Allegro

Op. 54, No. 4

Practice each note separately at first with the L. H. At N.B. raise the bow off the string during the rest to come up to the frog for the next stroke.

Op. 45, No. 6

Moderato

33

Moderato

34

30

Op. 54, No. 26

35

N.B. This "D" is located a half tone higher than the preceding A♭, (both played with the 3rd finger.)   The student
should bear this in mind during this and the subsequent studies in key of E♭ major (three flats)

24744-56

Allegro

Op. 45, No. 12

38

cover both strings

Allegro molto

Op. 54, No. 29

39

Allegro
W.B.

Op. 45, No. 20

40

cover both notes

ritenuto _ _ _ _ a tempo

ritenuto _ _ _ _ a tempo

molto   ritenuto

Preparatory Exercise for No. 41   The up-bow on the third beat should be a quick, sweeping stroke.

Allegro con fuoco

41   Count 1 2 3 4

Op. 74, No. 15

N.B. Cover both strings

86

Op. 54, No. 80

42

24744-56

The student should be careful to keep the time accurately in playing the quarter notes, as each quarter note should get the *full* time of a triplet i.e. *three eighth notes*.

Allegro non tanto

Op. 54, No. 17

43

Op. 45, No. 26

Allegro

Preparatory Exercise for No.45

The best way to work out this study is by slowly counting eight to a measure, so as to allow enough time to raise the bow off the string at the eighth rest, and start the next measure downbow again.

N.B. The student should note that the five measures beginning with the one marked N.B. are in the key of E♭ major (with three flats); these are followed by another three measures in the key of G major (with one sharp and all the flats cancelled.)

At first to be practiced with three notes to a stroke.

Allegro

Op. 54, No. 3

46

Preparatory Exercise for No. 48

Allegro

Op. 54, No. 5

48

Preparatory Exercise for No. 49

Tempo di Valse

Op. 54, No. 19

49

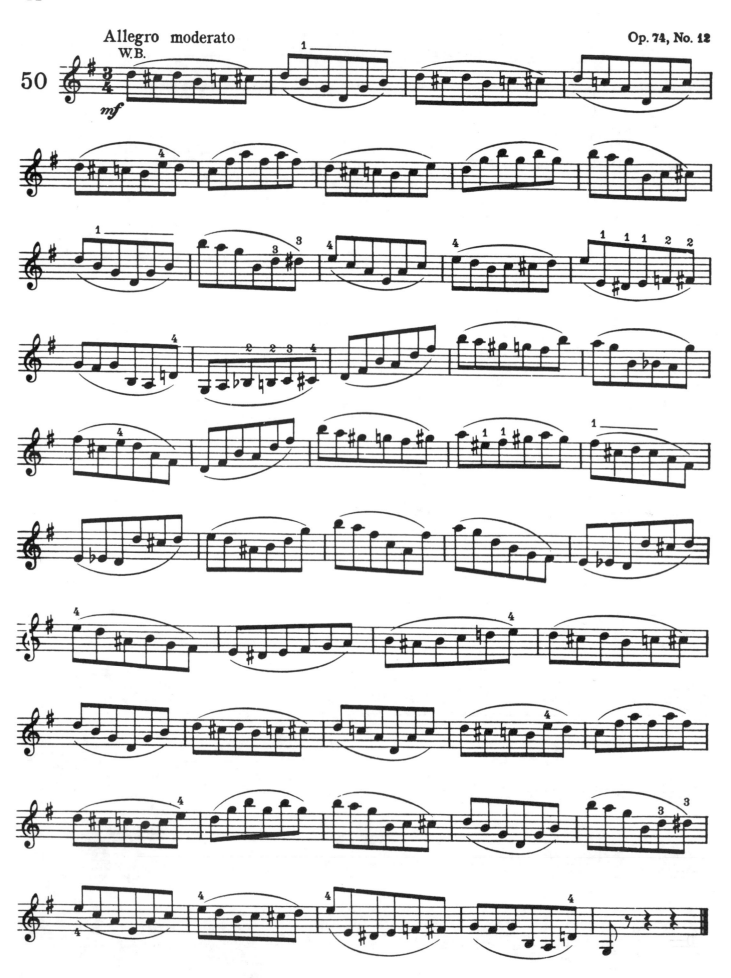

Allegro moderato
W.B.

50

Op. 74, No. 12

Variants to No. 51

Allegro moderato

Op. 74, No. 8

51

Andante sostenuto

Op. 54, No. 20

52

Moderato   Op. 45, No. 10

53

*) This "D" is located a half tone lower (on A string) than the preceding "G♯" on the D string. This fact should be born in mind throughout this study.

Allegro moderato   Op. 54, No. 28

54

Op. 74, No. 11

55

48

56 — Op. 54, No. 21

Allegretto   Op. 54, No. 25

U.H.

57

N.B. Play gradually slower, using *a little more* bow for up strokes which should bring the bow near the Frog by the time the final long note is reached

Presto

Op. 54, No. 24

58

Notes marked with (>) should be given full sweeping strokes.

Op. 54, No. 84

PRACTICE PLANNER

Date	Page	Goals/Comments	Remarks

Date	Page	Goals/Comments	Remarks

Jascha Heifetz Folios

"The Heifetz Collection" for Violin & Piano
A collection of twenty-four classic Heifetz transcriptions along with a bonus of two violin concerto cadenzas that are part of the legacy and legend of the "father of modern, virtuoso violin playing." This edition contains separate piano and violin parts, that are expertly edited, engraved and printed to provide many years of use and pleasure. Foreword by Itzhak Perlman.
(Cat. No. ATF116)

"New Favorite Encore Folio" for Violin & Piano
This fine collection of fifteen compositions was selected and edited by Heifetz and presented in outstanding engravings and printing. Compositions include "Rigaudon", "Zapateado," "Guitarre" in addition to pieces by Schubert, Mendelssohn, Mozart, Brahms and Schumann among others.
(Cat. No. O2137)

Jascha Heifetz

New
Favorite Encore Folio
for Violin and Piano

CARL FISCHER

FRITZ KREISLER
FOLIOS

The Fritz Kreisler Collection
for Violin & Piano

An outstanding edition of original compositions and transcriptions for violin and piano, as well as cadenzas. The collection includes twenty-two Kreisler favorites compiled by Eric Wen with a foreword by Yehudi Menuhin.
(Cat. No. ATF115)

The Fritz Kreisler Collection, Vol. 2
for Violin & Piano

A second collection consisting of thirty-five favorites and specialties. More transcriptions & arrangements and original compositions compiled by Eric Wen. Includes commentary and insights into Kreisler's technique.
(Cat. No. ATF124)

Favorite Encore Folios
for Violin & Piano

A collection of eleven compositions for violin and piano selected and edited by Kreisler. Includes "Tambourin," "Serenade du Tsigane" and pieces by Brahms, Bach, Bizet and Mendelssohn among others.
(Cat. No. O1290)

Eight Original Pieces and Arrangements
for Violin & Piano

A marvelous edition of simplified pieces from the pen of Kreisler. Contents include "Toy Soldiers March", "Rondino On A Theme" by Beethoven plus six other easy pieces for violin and piano.
(Cat. No. F3502)

VIOLIN BOOKS

◼ *AMBROSIO*

___ 02648 MINIATURE MASTERPIECES
    for Violin & Piano, Vol. 3
___ 02585 RELIGIOUS MEDITATIONS

◼ *BACH*

___ 029 10 LITTLE CLASSICS (Seely-Brown)

◼ *DE BERIOT*

___ 01249 METHOD, Op. 102 (Saenger), Part 1

◼ *BYTOVETSKI*

___ 03056 SCALE TECHNIC

◼ *DOUNIS*

___ 02695 ARTIST'S TECHNIC, Op. 12
___ 03378 HIGHER DEVELOPMENT OF THIRDS
    & FINGERED OCTAVES, Op. 30

◼ *DUNHAM*

___ 01453 FIDDLIN' DANCE TUNES

◼ *FOSS*

___ 05186 THREE AMERICAN PIECES

◼ *HOLMES-WEBBER*

___ 03807 ABOVE THE FIRST POSITION

◼ *LET US HAVE MUSIC FOR VIOLIN AND PIANO*

___ 03206 Volume 1
___ 03207 Volume 2

◼ *PAGANINI*

___ 03224 24 CAPRICES (Kross)

◼ *SITT*

___ 04215 20 STUDIES IN THE 6th AND 7th POSITIONS
    Op. 32, Book 4

◼ *WOHLFAHRT*

___ 02465 FOUNDATION STUDIES (Aiquoni) Book 1
___ 02466 FOUNDATION STUDIES (Aiquoni) Book 2
    50 EASY AND MELODIC STUDIES, Op. 74 (Sharp)

Selected Music for Violin from the
CARL FISCHER MUSIC LIBRARY

Violin Methods by the Masters

LEOPOLD AUER

GRADED COURSE OF VIOLIN PLAYING

From the master teacher of the "masters,"—the most comprehensive and valuable method written. For the quick and dedicated, or older student. Also highly recommended for the advancing Suzuki player for introduction to note reading.

Graded Course
O1416	Book 1—Preparatory
O1419	Book 2—Pre-Elementary
O1446	Book 3—Elementary
O1447	Book 4—Elementary, cont.
O1448	Book 5—Medium Advanced
O1449	Book 6—Advanced
O1450	Book 7—Difficult
O1451	Book 8—Virtuoso

MAIA BANG

VIOLIN METHOD

Based on the teaching principles of Leopold Auer. As sound and logical as when written, this time honored method is still "the" standard for beginning students. Utilizing Auer's principles Maia Bang's well-graded material provides ample exercises and songs at each level. This course of study leads the student to the development of solid technique and fine musicianship.

O42	Part 1—Elementary Rudiments (English ~ Spanish Texts)
O43	Part 2—More Advanced Studies
O44	Part 3—2nd ~ 3rd Positions
O45	Part 4—4th ~ 5th Positions
O46	Part 5—6th ~ 7th Positions
O47	Part 6—Higher Art of Bowing
O2498	Part 1—(English Text Only)

CARL FLESCH

O1317	THE ART OF VIOLIN PLAYING Book 1 — Technique in General and Applied Technique
O2046	Book 2 —Artistic Realization and Instruction
O205	BASIC STUDIES FOR VIOLIN
O2358	PROBLEMS OF TONE PRODUCTION IN VIOLIN PLAYING
O5188	SCALE SYSTEM Scale exercises in all major and minor keys

C.H. HOHMANN

PRACTICAL VIOLIN METHOD

O286	Book 1 —The open strings and preliminary exercises and pieces
O287	Book 2 — Exercises and pieces in the easiest keys
O288	Book 3 — Advanced exercises and pieces in all sharp and flat keys
O289	Book 4 — Exercises and pieces in the higher positions
O290	Book 5 — Exercises and pieces in the higher positions and of greater difficulty

GEORGE PERLMAN

O2779	THE VIOLINIST'S CONTEST ALBUM Fourteen compositions in the third position
	VIOLINISTS FIRST SOLO ALBUM
O2663	Vol. I-Elementary
O2664	Vol. 2-Intermediate
O4460	VIOLINIST'S RECITAL ALBUM A collection of stylistic solos

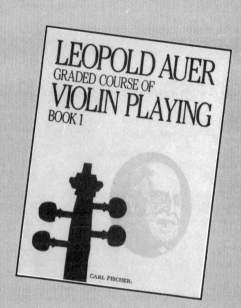